SHERE POVERTY

This little book gives a picture of a Surrey parish community at the beginning of the Georgian period, its size, the occupations of its members, the central position of the church and in particular the elaborate local organisation in place to support the poor. This offered payment for rent, regular weekly pensions for the elderly and widows, clothing, money for tools, even help with a marriage license and other incidentals (so that an expected child might be supported by its father, rather than the parish). The poor were put to work on spinning and weaving and apprenticeships were found for children. Until the 1790s householders in the parish who were assessed to pay the Poor Rate did not find this an intolerable burden.

All this changed with population growth, the beginning of industrialisation and inflation following the outbreak of the Napoleonic Wars. In Shere the parish officials suddenly found they had to face the new and difficult problem of unemployed, able-bodied men.

Nationally opinions were changing (giving money to the poor 'encouraged them to breed'), and it was felt necessary to change the system of poor relief from being parish based to being centrally controlled, from small parish workhouses to large Union workhouses serving several parishes.

How conditions in the parish of Shere changed over 150 years is described with a wealth of detail and family names taken from original records and illustrated with photographs, engravings, and copies of old documents.

SHERE POVERTY

From Parish Workhouse to Union Workhouse

by

ANN NOYES

TWIGA BOOKS
GOMSHALL

First published 1996
Reprinted 2006
© Ann Noyes

Twiga Books
Twiga Lodge
Wonham Way
Gomshall
Surrey GU5 9NZ

ISBN 0 9528625 0 6

Printed and bound by
IntypeLibra Ltd

Acknowledgements

This book is based on research for the Diploma in English Local History at Portsmouth Polytechnic (now Portsmouth University) in 1990 -1991. Thanks are due to Dr James Thomas and Barry Stapleton for the enthusiasm they generated and the methods they taught me. My thanks also go to the staff of the Surrey County Record Office and the Guildford Muniment Room. I am particularly indebted to John Janaway of the Surrey Local Studies Library for his encouragement and advice. 'Twiga' is the word for giraffe in Swahili and I am grateful to Duncan Mirylees of the Surrey Local Studies Libary for drawing the giraffe's head for the logo. My daughter Alice has offered her expertise on publishing and printing and the work would not have been completed without the help of my husband, Tom, who tamed the word processor and taught me some of its mysteries.

SHERE POVERTY

FROM PARISH WORKHOUSE TO UNION WORKHOUSE

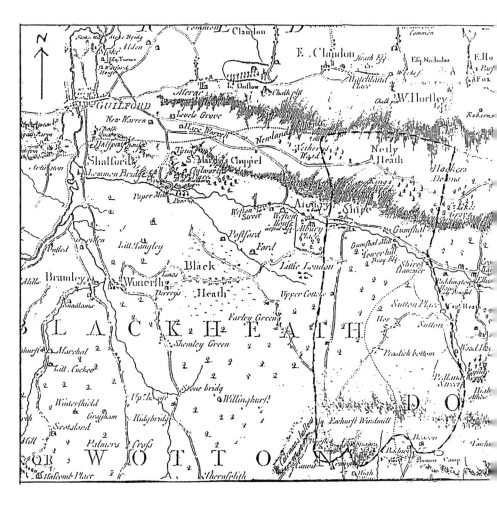

A section of John Seller's map of Surrey 1670 with approximate boundary of Shere Parish shown thus :------
Scale 1 inch to the mile reduced by 10%

The Parish of Shere in 1711

The rich man's wealth is his strong city: the destruction of the poor is their poverty
Proverbs

In the early eighteenth century Shere, Gomshall and their surrounding settlements formed a rural parish with a population of about 550 persons. They were concerned with growing crops and milling the corn; keeping sheep for spinning and weaving the wool; growing flax for linen; rearing cattle for meat and tanning the hides to produce leather for boots and harness. Many of the houses which survive today were already 200 years old.

The administration of poor relief was vested in the parish, through its voluntary Overseers who collected money in rates from those assessed to pay and gave relief in cash or kind to the elderly, the sick, the widows and the mothers of children born out of wedlock. This relief could be given in the workhouse, or at home as 'out-relief'.

At this time the situation seemed to be in balance. The number of poor receiving help was no more than one might reasonably expect and the rate payers were not unduly burdened. This situation changed radically during the course of the eighteenth century and this study aims to trace the process of change from the equilibrium of the early 1700s, through the crisis years around 1800 to the takeover by central government of the administration of poor relief after 1834. As a result of this, the poor in the parish of Shere were no longer accommodated in the local workhouse but in the large, institutional Union Workhouse in Guildford and out-relief was generally denied.

The parish of Shere is in the south west of the county of Surrey, with its northern boundary on the crest of the North Downs, its southern boundary on the greensand of the Hurtwood, with the fertile valley of the Tillingbourne between. As well as the village of Shere it encompasses Gomshall, part of Holmbury St. Mary (formerly Pitland Street), Hoe, Peaslake and also scattered farms. The top slopes of the chalk Downs offered grazing for sheep, the valley bottom was used for pasture and meadow. The fields between supported arable cultivation and the poor soils of the greensand were the source of wood and peat for fuel.

The population of the parish grew from 550 in 1725 to 871 in 1801 and had risen to 1190 in 1831, more than doubling in 100 years. These numbers would include a higher proportion of children and a lower proportion of elderly people than there are today. An analysis of the burial register for 1717 to 1766 shows infants and 'sons and daughters', understood to be children living at home with parents, making up nearly half of the entries. From the same source and for the same dates, 10% are classed as 'poor'. The rural nature of the parish is illustrated by the entries the Rev. George Duncomb, rector of Shere 1714-1746 and the Rev. Thomas Duncomb, rector 1746-1764, made in the burial register and which gave the occupations of their parishioners at death.   The number of times each occupation was mentioned in the 50 year period is tabulated overleaf.

blacksmith	4	farmer	4
weaver	1	gardener	1
labourer	26	tailor	1
thatcher	2	bricklayer	1
husbandman	10	writing master	1
yeoman	8	carpenter/joiner	4
traveller	5	tanner	2
servant	10	cordwainer	1
butcher	4	miller	1
maltman/maltster	2	higgler	1
innholder	3	collarmaker	1
cooper	1		

Yeoman and husbandmen were both landholders, as owners or tenants, yeoman had a higher status; a cordwainer worked with leather, usually shoemaking; a higgler was an itinerant dealer, generally with a horse and cart. It is surprising that 'miller' is only mentioned once, as more than one mill is known to have been working during the period, but the classification made by the Duncombs will reflect the perceptions of the time, and it is likely that those engaged in milling appear as yeomen. There is no mention of a baker, but bread must have been baked in several houses in the villages. Bread and hard cheese were the staple food of the poor.

Shere was an 'open parish', not one dependent on a noble family. There were few gentry families; the Brays had held at least one of the manors, and sometimes all four, from 1485 and still hold them today. William Bray, whose life span almost matches that of this study, lived from 1736 to 1832. He was a solicitor and historian, co-author of *The History and Antiquities of the County of Surrey* published between 1804 and 1811. He had a home in London but latterly lived in the parish. In the early Vestry Book the first assessment of 1711 lists 115 ratepayers of which only the names of Edward Bray and Peter Hussey are designated as 'esquire' for Shere and Gomshall. The Right Honourable Lord Garnsey and George Duncomb Esq. of Albury are classed as 'Out Parishioners'; at that time parcels of land in Albury parish belonged to the parish of Shere.

This study starts from the year 1711, as that is the date of the first Overseers' Account Book to have survived and continues to 1841, shortly after Shere Workhouse was sold as a result of the implementation of the Poor Law Amendment Act of 1834. This amalgamated parishes into Unions and placed the administration of Union Workhouses in the hands of Guardians who were responsible to centrally appointed Poor Law Commissioners. Shere was included in the Guildford Union. Poor relief was thereafter to be restricted to those in the workhouse, apart from exceptional cases. The Union Workhouse in Guildford later became St. Luke's Hospital.

'The Poor' are hard to define at any time and at this period few were literate and thus able to leave records of their lives, although the Widow Stocker was able to make her needs known, as will be seen later. They were known in Shere by their requests for help to the Vestry, the governing body of the parish and to the overseers of the poor, who left a detailed account of the disbursements they made in money and cloth and rent. In the Burial Register of the eightenth century, the Rectors might add the comment 'a poor man' as they mentioned other occupations.

The period under review was a time of accelerating change in British society, with the growth of industrialisation, changes in agricultural practice and rapid population growth from the middle of the eighteenth century. As the main areas of industrial development were in the Midlands and the North of England, prosperity ebbed from the South and agricultural wages fell in relation to the price of bread, so that a man in work could barely support his family and any untoward event, such as illness or an accident, or the birth of a baby, could tip the family into poverty. There are several examples in the overseers' account books of payment given to a family 'in sickness' indicating an exceptional circumstance.

The Square, Shere, with the *White Horse* centre left where the Vestry Meetings were sometimes held

The Old Poor Law

Blessed is he that considereth the poor
Isaiah

The system of care for those unable to support themselves, collectively called 'poor' but in effect the elderly, the sick, the widows, orphans and the mothers of bastard children, was vested in the Parish by the Elizabethan Poor Laws of 1597-1601. There was a need to fill the void after the dissolution of the Monasteries in the 1530s had removed a previous source of support. These laws established a pattern of parish responsibility; all owners and occupiers of land and property were assessed according to the size of their holding and the parish vestry would then 'set a rate' (of so many old pence in the pound) which had to be approved by the Justices of the Peace. The parish officers, who served in a voluntary capacity, would announce this rate by a notice on the church door, collect the money and disburse it to the poor according to need. Poor people would apply to the Vestry for help, and in a small community, the conditions of the applicants would be known and understood. The overseers kept a careful account of income and expenditure, made up the books annually and handed over the responsibility and any balance to their successors at the Easter Vestry.

Entries covering the first years of the earliest Vestry Book give a clear picture of the problems encountered in village life at the beginning of the Georgian period, and how they were tackled. The church is shown to be the place where parish meetings were held, decisions made and orders published. There were regular 'pensioners' and others whose rent was paid; and there were those who received relief at times of special hardship. Parishioners were paid for looking after sick neighbours and funeral expenses could be covered. Parish responsibilities are set out clearly in the preamble to the monthly meeting:-

At A monthly meeting of the Churchwardens and Overseers of the poore and other Inhabitants of the parish of Sheere touching the Reliefe of the poore of the same parish in their parish Church on Sunday the 9th day of September Annoq^e Dm 1711 In the afternoons after Divine Service it is ordered as followeth by us whose names are hereunto subscribed

Ordered that an Assensm^t be made within the said parish for Raysing the some of £48 15s 5d (£48.77) being for and towards the Reliefe of the poore of the said parish and for the placeing forth of poore Children App^rntice etc and for the buying of A Conveinent stocke therein to sett the poore thereof on worke And for the Reembursing of the Churchwardens and Overseers of the poore all such moneys as have been by them disbursed for the purposes aforesaid which Assensm^t is agreed to be for six months ending the first day of October

It is also ordered that the sev^rall poore people hereunder written be allowed weekly the Respective sumes of Money hereunder written for and towards their Reliefe

	s. d.	p
Edward Spicer, ye weeke	3. 0.	15
Dorothy Hueber	1. 6.	7
Widow Caplen	2. 0.	10
John Holney	2. 0.	10
Widow Constable	1. 0.	5
Widow Street	1. 0.	5
Widow Beldham	1. 6.	7
Widow Tickner	1. 6.	7
George Laker	3. 0.	15
Margaret Pricklove	1. 0.	5
John Blasden	2. 0.	10
John Hind	1. 0.	5

[Signed By]

Nathaniel Woods
Richard Coe
John Holland
John Nye
William Jeffrey

John Russell,	Churchwarden
John Stevens,	- do -
John Wakeford,	Overseer of the Poor
John Harding,	- do -

The Assessment ordered at this meeting in September, to raise money retrospectively to cover expenditure since May, was applied to fifty landholders in Shere, fifty in 'the Libertie of Gumshall, Hoe and Sutton' and fifteen Out Parishioners. Only fourteen of this total paid over one pound. The rate was seven pence (3p) in the pound and was approved by Justices of the Peace Edward Bray and Peter Hussey on 15th September 1711. Another rate was collected on 4th April 1712 and the sum of the two rates was £104. 9s. 1½d. (£104.46).

The Churchwardens and Overseers gave a summary account of receipts and expenditure during the year 1711-12, (years ran from March 25th until 1752), and the custom of keeping the accounting year from Easter to Easter continued, as it still does. They record nine widows, six men and one 'poor maid' being allowed weekly sums of between 4s.(20p) and 1s. (5p) per week. One year's rent was paid on behalf of eleven widows and nine men but it is the single payments and the policy of subsidising neighbourly acts which highlight the human situations. Eight shillings (40p) were 'given to the Widow Bowbrick for Relief in sickness' but also two shillings (10p) for 'tending of the Widow Bowbrick'. There were four entries for 'tending of the Widow Capelin', and in the following year 6s.10½d. (37p) was paid out for 'washing of Goody Caplan's Cloathes'. 'Pd for mending of the well rope for old Blasden' would seem to be a welcome act for maintaining an old man's independence. A series of entries concern the Widow Reeves:-

	s. d.	p
given to Widow Reeves for relief	4. 1.	21
pd to Mary Kelsey for laying her forth	1. 0.	5
pd for the Affidavit & the makeing of him	1. 0.	5
pd for the coffin and shroud	10. 0.	50
pd for bread and cheese at her burial	5. 5.	27
pd to Elizabeth Kelsey for tending her	4. 0.	20
pd for the burying of her	2. 2.	11

Subsequently Mary Reeves needed help; was she a handicapped daughter adrift without her widowed mother's care? She was well supported by the parish as the following entries show:-

	£ s d	p.
pd for a pair of stockings for Mary Reeves	9	4
pd for a pair of bodices for her	2. 6	13
pd for two hemd herchiefs for her	1. 0	5
pd for my keeping of her 10 weeks	1. 19. 0	£1.90
pd for a pair of shoes for her	2. 6	13
pd for a pair of pattens for her	1. 0	5
pd to Willi Woods for keeping of her 1 month	4. 0	20
pd to Thomas Redford for keeping of her 5 months	1. 0. 0	£1

Pair of 19th. Century Pattens with wooden soles. The oval shaped irons are mounted on short legs & are riveted to the sole at front and back. The toe caps and side pieces are made of leather.

Other entries relate to a small outlay for the provision of tools which would help a man to work and earn:-

| pd for a sickle for Jno Steer | 1s. 0d. | 5p |
| pd for a knife for Thos. Street | 4d. | 2p |

Parish Church of St. James, Shere

Elizabethan Poor Law gave an additional responsibility to the parish overseers; that of providing work where none was available, as mentioned in the preamble to the parish meeting quoted above. The overseers of Shere made an effort to put this into effect. They bought flax and paid for the spinning and weaving and then distributed the linen as piece lengths or clothes for the poor. In 1719 the Vestry Book records:- 'An account of ye Broad and Narrow Cloth that is Wove by Richard Stone and John Stone. The material that John and Richard wove was distributed to the poor and accounted for by the parish clerk in his 'Account of the Narrow and Broad Cloth that is Linnen given in by Henry Mellersh before the Inhabitants of the parish of Sheere.'

It was distributed to named recipients, the majority of whom are subsequently mentioned in the burial register as 'poor', in lengths of so many Ells. An English Ell was 45 inches, narrow cloth was 45 inches wide or less and broad cloth could be up to two yards wide. There are records of payments 'for 6 pounds of flax 3/- (15p)' in 1711-12 and also 'for spining of 6 pounds of Flax 3/- (15p)' and 'for makeing of the Poores cloathes 12/9. (64p)' The entry which recorded an outlay of one shilling (5p) to George Laker 'to get him from us' seemed to have failed in its purpose as a later entry reads 'pd for makeing of George Laker 2 shirts 1s.(5p)' and 'pd for the D[r] for George Laker 16s.(80p)'. He died ten years later in the parish and was described as 'an ancient poor man'.

The duty of 'placeing forth poore children App[r]ntice etc', mentioned above is carried on throughout the period; 'pd with Lemans boy an App[r]ntice £2(£2.00)' and 'pd to Henry Wakeford with John Venn put to him as Apprentice £4(£4.00)'. Both these were in 1711-12 but later there are records of fines charged to those unwilling to take on an apprentice.

Insights into personal possessions can be gained from a group of Inventories recorded between 1726 and 1728 and at no other time. It would seem to be another duty of the overseers of the poor to collect and list items after a death, and if no other provision had been made, to distribute these goods to others in need. Thus:-

> An Inventory of the Goods sent to William Baker for the use of Thos. Wilds children on August ye 23 1726 by Mr Braye.
> pt. of Old Ede Goods
> One Feather Bed, Two Bollsters, Two Pillows, one coverlid, Four Blankets and one pair of Sheets

and:

> An Inventory of Dorothy Hookers Goods Late Deceased taken February ye 16th 1726 by Edward Bray Esq.and Jno. Harding:
>
> One Flock Bed and Bedstettle, Mat and Cord, One Chest, One Table, Two Chairs,
> One Iron Pot, One Brass Kettle,
> Four Shifts, One Gound (gown), One Peticoat and some old Headclothes
>
> Memorandum Ann Hart Recd Doris Hookers caps W[d] Spicer 1 Shift
> 1727 Aug 22 W[d] Spicer Recd 2 Shifts
> 1728 April 13 Ann Hart Recd her Hatt and ye wid Bignold 1 Shift.
>
> Ann Hart 'of the workhouse' was buried on December 28th 1730.

The Inventory of Widow Amey, taken on December 11th 1727 indicates that she was a woman of some property. She had ample utensils in her kitchen for open hearth cooking, and also 'One Settle, one Table, 1 Dresser, 2 Candlesticks, Ten dishes of White Wear (ware) and 3 Chairs'. There was also a Parlour containing a form, a chair and a sideboard, two beds in the 'kitchen chamber', a back room and a brewery.

These quotations from the earliest Vestry Book cover the years 1711 to 1728, which includes the period in which the Shere Parish Workhouse was built, as described in the next chapter. There are no detailed Poor Law Account Books extant from 1728 until 1776; from that year the records resume, and continue with a few omissions until 1821.

Apart from the regular collection and distribution of the Poor Rate there were in addition some 'Charitable Benefactions to the Parish of Shere' funded from the interest on money invested or by rents from land or property donated to the Parish. The declared purposes were to provide bread for poor widows, for teaching poor children to read, for an annual sermon, and to the poor receiving no weekly pay. One was left to the discretion of the Trustees, who were the Rector and Churchwardens. The total 'annual produce' was £32.9s.2d. (£32.46) in 1786, less than a tenth of the amount raised in poor rates at the time.

From 1711 until the 1790s there did not appear to be a problem in Shere with those unable to find work, and the overseers accounts showed that the amounts needed to support the elderly and the infirm did not represent an undue burden on the parish ratepayers. In 1776 one of the monthly accounts shows a total expenditure of £18.0s.2d. (£18.01). This included bills for goods and services for the paupers in the workhouse and out-relief to three widows, four mothers of bastards, William Jones senior, and one family at a cost of £3.13s.6d. (£3.67). The total collected for the year 1776-77 was £385.2s.5d. (£385.12) from two rates of two shillings (10p) in the pound.

CHARITABLE BENEFACTIONS to the Parish of SHIRE, as returned to Parliament, 1786.

Name of the Person who gave the Charity ; and how and when given.	Whether in Land or Money, and for what Purpose given.	In whom now vested.	Amount, if in Money. £. s. d.	Annual Produce. £. s. d.
Mr. Smith, by will, 1625.	In Land.—To Poor receiving no weekly Pay.	Trustees, God schall Esq. Budgen Esq. &c. &c.		10 0 0¹
Mr. Gatton, by will, 1758.	Money, 400l. which purchased 457l. three per Cent. — To educate poor children of the Parish, and an annual Sermon.	Trustees, Rev. Mr. Duncomb, Mr.Shurlock,Mr. Woods.		13 14 2¹
Mr.Duncomb, by will, 1746.	In Land.—For bread for the Poor of Shire and Albury, and teaching poor children to read.	Rector of Shire.		6 0 0
Mrs.CharityDuncomb by will, unknown.	In Land in the Parish of Cranley.— Weekly distribution of bread for poor Widows.	Churchwardens.		1 6 0
Mr. Maybank, by will, 1667.	In Land in the Parish of Cranley.— To the Poor of Shire.	Churchwardens.		0 14 0⁵
Francis Haybitle, by will, 1784.	House in Shire.—To the Poor of Shire.	Officers of the Parish.		0 15 0⁶
				£.32 9 2

THOMAS DUNCUMB, Rector.
WILLIAM SHURLOCK, } Churchwardens.
JOHN MAYBANK, }

From Manning & Bray *History and Antiquities of the County of Surrey*, Vol. I. (1804)

From the last decade of the eighteenth century the parish faced the new problem of having to provide for unemployed able-bodied men. Nationally, the changes which led to this situation included the amalgamation of small farms to form bigger units (thus easier for the landlord to collect the rent and for farmers to introduce new agricultural practices), and a subtle alteration in the way farmers perceived themselves. They tended to distance themselves from their servants and this led to a reduction in the custom of living-in farm servants sharing the family board, and the increase in the hiring of casual labour; thus young men without a family farm would be deprived of a stable period of about ten years of employment and training. William Cobbett observed in a characteristically pungent comment that 'When farmers became gentlemen then labourers became slaves'. The effect of the Revolutionary and Napoleonic wars from 1793 to 1815 made for increased hardship among those then designated as 'the lower orders', coupled with concern in Government that revolutionary practices abroad might be copied in England. Men without work were thought to be a threat to good order and public reaction was harsh and condemning. Wheat prices increased as imported corn was restricted during the wars so that bread, the staple food, was expensive and wages fell, especially agricultural wages in the South.

The principle of subsidising wages from the poor rates was established by magistrates at Speen in 1795 and became known as the Speenhamland system. Wages could be topped up in relation to the price of bread and the numbers of children in a family. This system may have been devised in a spirit of good will but its effects were adverse. Employers would dismiss skilled men for whom they had to pay a full wage in favour of those whose wages were partly paid by the parish and the burden on the rate payers was increased. Surrey was not considered to be one of the Speenhamland counties, and no identifiable record of wage subsidy in Shere parish exists although 'family allowances' were common.

The combination of unemployed able-bodied men and adverse weather in 1799 and 1800 produced crisis conditions in the parish of Shere. In both years there was exceptionally bad weather and consequent poor harvests, at a time when a rural community lived from harvest to harvest and there were few reserves. For 1799 it was reported that 'from its commencement to its close this season was, perhaps, as ungenial to the productions of the earth and to the animal creation as any upon record, and the inclemency extended over a great part of Europe. In 1800 'Wheat 113s. 10d (£5.69) a quarter, a consequence mostly of the previous wet summer. Another disappointing harvest'. Wheat had cost 38s.2d. (£1.91) in 1776. A comment written by the economist Joseph Lowe in 1823 reinforces this observation:- 'The summer of 1799 was wet, and it unfortunately happened, as in 1796, that large purchases of corn were necessary . . . Matters would then have improved . . . had not the calamity of a deficient harvest taken place in 1800, and raised the price of corn to an unexampled height. The total value of our corn imports during 1800, 1801 and part of 1802, was declared in evidence before a parliamentary committee to be no less than £15,000,000 sterling'.

The population in the parish had grown from 827 in 1784 to 871 at the first census of 1801, a 5% increase, but the numbers of those in receipt of poor relief outside the workhouse increased from nine to 93, and of those, 72 were men. The majority of these were likely to be heads of households and breadwinners for their wives and families.

In February 1801 there is a record of 'Weekly Allowances to sundry Poor Labourers of the parish of Shiere in consideration of the present extraordinary high prices, Provisions to commence the 8th February 1801'. This lists 25 men and the numbers of their children who would receive cash, potatoes, rice and bacon. It is no wonder that the aggregate rate set (from four tranches), was 22s.(£1.10) in the pound and the amount collected from the 84 rate payers in the parish reached a total of £1,444.11s.0d. (£1,444.55).

These figures show the rapid change in demand from 1776-1801, and although the situation in Shere eased somewhat after that year , it never returned to the balanced condition of 1776. There were always many unemployed men receiving out-relief, although noticeably fewer in the summer months when casual labour was easier to find. The distress of those unable to find work and feed their families must have been mirrored by the anxiety on the part of the local ratepayers concerned with the greatly increased level of payments, although farmers were receiving more for their corn as prices were enhanced.

One further duty fell upon the overseers of the poor which caused a considerable outlay of time and expense. This was in consequence of the recommendations of the Act of Settlement of 1662. Before this date the poor who were able and willing to work were free to move about the country in search of employment, only those not so able and willing were obliged to stay in their parish of settlement. Expanding parishes would be glad of extra labour, but no parish would welcome those likely to be a charge upon the Poor Rates; the sick, the elderly and the bastard child, and great efforts were made to exclude them.

Right of settlement was gained by birth in the parish, by apprenticeship and by employment. Marriage offered settlement to a woman from another parish, a man did not acquire automatic settlement rights by moving to the parish of his wife's birth. Another route to settlement was renting a £10 tenement or holding office in the parish. Removal to the previous parish of settlement was practised if an incomer claimed relief, and a system of certification grew up by which a man might travel to seek work in another parish, and be accepted there, so long as he held a certificate which showed that his parish of origin agreed to accept responsibility if he should become pauperised.

Part of a form of 1757: Elizabeth Lemmon, resident in Shere had settlement rights in Dorking.

The Accompts of Mr. William — Shurlock and Mr. John Tanner

Overseers of the Poor of the Parish of Shiere — of all Money By them Received and

Disbursed from the 26 day of May 1776 to — the 14 day of May 1777.

Mr. Shurlocks Accompts

	£	s	d
Received of the last Overseers	29	19	2¼
By the first Rate	82	15	.
By the second Rate	83	.	.
Rec the Annuity Money from Cranley	2	.	.
	197	14	2¼

Mr. Tanners Accompts

	£	s	d
Received of the last Overseers	29	19	2¼
By the first Rate	78	19	.
By the second Rate	78	10	.
	187	8	2¼

Paid

		£	s	d
1776 May 6 as by this Months Account		18	.	2
July 21 as by Do		14	19	10¼
September 15 Do		13	4	10¼
November 10 Do		26	3	11
1777 January 5 Do		26	13	3
March 2 Do		38	8	6
April 27 Do		18	5	7
Paid Dr. Newland a Bill		7	9	9
Uncollected of John Bristow		0	8	0
Do of Charlywoorth		0	8	0
Vestry Clerk a years Sallary Due at Christ last		1	4	.
Paid him a Bill		.	6	6
Pd for keeping account of Smith's Money entering in the Book and Copy for Mr Bray		.	5	.
Pd receiving Money from Cranley		.	1	.
Pd the Church Wardens their Accounts		.	14	8
Paid Willj's Expences the Coroner and his Inquest holding the death of Bristow's Child		.	15	3
Pd Expences giving up Church Wardens & Overseers Accompt		.	10	.
		183	12	4
In Hand		14	1	10½

William Shurlock

Paid

		£	s	d
1776 June 23 as by this Months Account		18	3	2
August 18 as by Do		17	1	1
October 13 Do		23	12	9
December 8 Do		25	14	4
1777 February 2 Do		24	5	3
March 30 Do		38	1	4
Paid Widow Diddle a Bill		.	7	.
My own Bill		3	3	6
Henry Hersey a Bill		.	9	.
Uncollected of the Widow Edser 2 Books		.	6	.
		151	2	11
In Hand		36	5	3½
Mr. Shurlock in Hand		14	1	10½
Total in hand £		50	7	1½

Thomas the Tanner Received 25 3 7

Henry Hunt Received 25 3 6¼

John Tanner

Joseph Coulton

(Geo) Cancey

Henry Hunt

Wm Chisman

Thomas Mialls jun

George Francis

There are several entries in the overseers account books and surviving copies of letters which show the extent of parish responsibilities for those of Shere parish now living away and claiming relief and also for those living within its boundaries but having settlement elsewhere. Over a period of 40 years, from 1780 to 1820, the overseers were in touch with their counterparts in 40 different parishes and money had to change hands at a time when coin was in short supply and many commercial transactions were carried out through bills of exchange. The majority of parishes in correspondence lay in Surrey but there was also mention of those as far afield as Tintern, Lymington and Newcastle-on-Tyne.

There are many examples from the parish of Shere that will illustrate the scale and complexity of the problem and the fact that there were printed forms in use show how commonly it occurred. One of these forms concerns Elizabeth Lemmon, a single women considered to be a burden to the parish of Shere which held no responsibility for her as her place of settlement was Dorking. Another example, which had to be taken to the Court of Common Pleas for resolution, concerned a 'militia family'. The local militia was embodied to relieve regular regiments for overseas service during the Napoleonic Wars, with a quota being laid upon each parish. If the man allotted to serve was unable or unwilling to do so he could recruit a substitute and there are records of quite large sums being paid out for this purpose; as in March 1804, 'Henry Nye towards the Hire of his Substitute by order £13.0.0.' Whoever served, there was a risk of his wife and family being a charge upon the parish. For example:-

In the year 1798 a man of the Parish of Ewhurst in Surrey, being drawn by Lot to serve in the Surrey Supplementary Militia, hired, as a Substitute, a person of the parish of Shiere in the same county, who had a wife and 4 children - The substitute was duly enrolled to serve in the Militia, and received his Bounty, and his wife and Family becoming a charge upon Shiere the order of a Justice was made on that Parish for Payment to the Substitutes Family of 7s. 6d.(37p) weekly (the usual allowance) with an Order at the same time on Ewhurst to reimburse these payments agreeable to the Statute.

The arrangement worked well for about a year, until the Ewhurst officers, discovering that the man had deserted, stopped further payments to Shere, while Shere continued to maintain the family. The Shere officers subsequently published an 'Advertisement for [the man's] Apprehension' and found that ' he is now in gaol for an offence committed by him against the Game Laws'. Judgement was in favour of Shere :-

as it appears in this case that the Parish of Shiere not knowing of such desertion had paid considerable sums of money. I think Ewhurst is bound to repay them all that they paid whilst they were ignorant that the man had left the regiment and if they refuse to pay such money the parish officers on demand a Refusal might be indicted for disobedience of the Order.

Common Pleas Westminster July 20th 1800

Up to the end of the the period of the Old Poor Law the agricultural labourer and the poor widow felt that they had a right to their allowances from the parish. They could go to the Justice of the Peace if they had a grievance, and if they could prove need the overseers were instructed, on a printed form, to arrange payment, as in the case of Thomas Jones in 1813 and Edward Gates in December 1831. Edward Gates had suffered a family tragedy in September of that year, as the overseers record that they paid Mr Davey, Surgeon, for attending an inquest on Edward Gates child burnt to Death a fee of £1.1s.(£1.05)

Widow Stocker was living in Midhurst, Sussex, from 1821 to 1831, with Settlement rights in Shere. She may have benefited from the charitable bequest 'for teaching poor children to read', as she has a trenchant style of writing in support of the claim for 'my pay':-

Sir as I have not heard from you I must remind you of my Pay which I am in great want of there is now Nine Week Due to me - I hope you will not Fail sending as soon as possible as I am in great want
I am Sirs your Humble servant   C Stocker

PS I must again beg you will not fail sending in a Day or Two my Pay being so small that I scarse know how to shift so longe if you could send it oftener I shuld be glad with

The overseers, men of the village with their own family and work responsibilities, must have found their year of office a demanding time. It is hoped they had full support from the Rector, the Churchwardens, the parish clerk and other members of the Vestry.

The Shere Workhouse

Rattle his bones over the stones
He's only a pauper whom nobody owns.
'The Pauper's Drive'
Thomas Noel, 1799-1861

There was a seventeenth century cottage at the west end of Upper Street, Shere, known as 'Allens' which was the parish house of Shere, in trust for the use of the poor, from 1697 until 1802. The Workhouse proper was purpose built in the early 1720s, at Peaslake, then known as Pislick Bottom and it still survives as two cottages. It was built in response to the Act of 1722-23.

This Act provided:- 'that the overseers and churchwardens with the consent of the majority of the inhabitants might purchase or hire buildings and contract with any person for lodging, keeping, maintaining and employing the poor. Persons refusing to enter the workhouse were to lose all their title to relief.' The clause decreeing that relief was to be dependent on entry to the workhouse was not observed in Shere and seemed to have been generally disregarded; it was overturned by Gilbert's Act of 1776, which allowed relief to be given out-of-doors. The concept of relating relief to residence in the workhouse was one of the main planks of the Poor Law Amendment Act over 100 years later in 1834.

The first mention of the workhouse is in copies of some letters the Rector enclosed with his answers to a set of questions that the Bishop of Winchester asked all his clergy to complete in 1724-25. The Bishop comments:-

Mr Duncomb encloses copies of letters which he has written to his Churchwardens and Overseers touching their new Poorhouse. He added 'whence only a miracle can cause the impotent poor to come to church (it being three miles distant)'.

Also in 1725, beside the name of Thomas Rutter who was buried on April 22nd, is the word 'inmate', the only time that term appears.

There is an early reference in the Vestry Book to building materials for the Workhouse:-

1728 2 April Memorandum
Then Agreed with Mr Chitty to Deliver to ye Workhouse at Sheer at Twenty five shillings (£1.25) for Two Thousand of Brick and further Agreed wth him for Thirteen shillings (65p) per Thousand for what more is wanting and to fetch the same our Selves and for Tyles at Fifteen shillings (75p) per Thousand for the same at the Kiln

Later in the century the Rev. Thomas Duncomb records against several names in the burial register as 'from the Workhouse', including Susan Honey, who was buried in 1794 after '40 years in Shere Workhouse'.

The Workhouse is built of Bargate stone, with brick dressings, under a pitched roof with a first storey and an attic storey. There are four bays and a central chimney and a two bay section of similar construction and date at the back which is said to have contained a mortuary. It was equipped for twenty residents according to the Inventory in 1836, though there would have been a fluctuating population, from Susan Honey's 40 years which was worthy of special note, to the single mothers being accommodated for their lying in, and the stranger 'sick on the road'.

Apart from the mention of the bricks and tiles in the first Vestry Book, there is, disappointingly, no record of negotiating for the site, although land subsequently taken into use for a garden was described as being 'of the waste of Mr Bray's manor;' neither is there any account of building or equipping the House and no payments made up to 1728 can be directly related to the running of it. This is in contrast to the Workhouse in the neighbouring village of Albury, which is of similar design, built in 1732 and for which a detailed account of bills paid for its construction survive. It was smaller than that at Peaslake, being equipped for twelve paupers plus the Governor or Governess and the total cost was £339.18s.4½d. (£339.92)

Shere Workhouse c.1724 - 1836

From 1776 the items in the overseers' account books provide circumstantial evidence but no record of numbers or cost per head, as appears later. There are, however, in the accounts for 1778 records of 'meat to the Workhouse £1.1s.0d. (£1.05), five hundred faggots to the Workhouse at £3.5s.0d. (£3.25)', a 'Fat hog' at £7.18s.2d. (£7.91) and a 'Bushell of Pease' at 5s.(25p). Through the years there is mention of meat, milk, a lamb, a sheep, a tub of pork, beef and bacon, wheat and yeast. There are also entries concerning loads of turf (or peat, for cooking and heating), and money gained from the 'poors work'. Mr Bray was paid 2s.(60p) Quit Rent for the Workhouse annually. Quit rent was 'a payment made by tenants to their lord to excuse themselves from the customary manor services'. It was not abolished until 1922.

John Ellyott's name appears in 1778, being paid £1.4s.0d. (£1.20) for 3 months service and in 1780 he is styled 'Elliott the Governor', but the sums to maintain the poor in the Workhouse are not specified; they must be covered by such entries as 'Mr Harris a Bill' and as David Harris was the Miller at Gomshall Mill to 1786 this indicates a supply of flour for bread. Mrs Pellate succeeded as governor in 1781, but her wage for 3 months service was 12s.(60p), half that received by John Elliott.

In July 1784 there was a meeting concerning 'Letting the Workhouse', and for the next year each month has an entry 'Thomas Hornsby (or Hornsbey) for keeping poor people one month'. The money he received works out at 2s.6d (12p) per person per week; numbers are specified and occupation varied between twelve and twenty. This was the system known as 'farming the workhouse' in which the person appointed purchased the provisions and made what he could from careful (or over-zealous) management. Thomas Hornsby served until August 1785 when Mrs Pellate returned at 4s.(20p) a month and the Bills were paid by the overseers. James Gadd was governor from August 1786 to May 1789, managing the workhouse at a rate of 2s.3d.(11p) per person per week, the numbers being between fifteen and twenty.

For the next thirteen years there was a succession of men engaged to manage the workhouse and out-relief on a fixed sum, so that no names of parishioners in receipt of relief or numbers in the workhouse are recorded. Thomas Brooks was active for three years, his successors Collyer and Vizard, for two and a half years, followed by John Etherington and William Edser, who only lasted a matter of months. Then the parish officers had to take up the burden again. From 1802-03 stability returned, though numbers of inmates were high and charges increased. In June 1802 there were 31 persons in the Workhouse (and this should have been the month for haymaking) at a charge of 3s.3d.(17p) per head per week. Numbers fluctuated between seventeen and 33 over the next twelve years, then reached a peak of 44 in 1819 when it must have been grossly overcrowded. Costs were steady at 4s.(20p) a week from 1810 to 1820, after that they started to come down.

Medical attention was provided for the poor in and out of the workhouse as in March 1780 the Overseers record that they 'Paid Doctor Borer for 1 year Looking after the Poor £6.6s (£6.30)' This must have been a retaining fee. The doctor asked for payment for specific treatment as instanced in July 1779, 'John Reffell towards the Doctors Bill acc^t of Thos Reffell's Wife's Broken Leg £2.2s.(£2.10)'.

Later, in 1832, there is a detailed proposal of charges by Mr Davey, Surgeon:-

To attend and supply with medicine including vaccination the Poor of the Parish
at per annum   £25.0s.0d.   £25.00
Out parishioners residing more than five miles from ye Parish Church and not
exceeding 7 to be charged 1/-(5p) per mile extra.
Medicine included in the 1/-(5p) per mile
Midwifery within the parish and out parishioners not exceeding 5 miles from
Parish Church each at   10s.6d.   53p
Midwifery exceeding five miles and not more than 7
from parish Church per mile extra   £1.0s.0d.   £1.00
Compound Fracture Thigh including medicine & attendance   £5.5s.0d   £5.25
Leg and Arm ditto   £3.3s.0d.   £3.15
Fracture Thigh and Leg   £3.3s.0d.   £3.15
Arm   £2.2s.0d.   £2.10
Ribs   £1.1s.0d.   £1.05

Neighbours were also called in to nurse and treat the sick; for example:- 'Webb for Mary Coles and bleeding her, 4s.6d.(23p)' in 1780. There was an outbreak of Smallpox in the villages in the 1790s and several entries make reference to help in nursing and in money terms. There was a Midwife, perhaps more than one, called in to deliver the children of the poor. Charges were 5s.(25p) or 7s.6d.(37p). 'Laying' , or laying-out the dead was another neighbourly duty undertaken, usually by a widow, at a fee of 5s.(25p). Single pregnant women would be delivered in the workhouse and spend their period of lying-in there.

The overseers seemed prepared to go to considerable trouble and expense to find the fathers of single pregnant women and arrange a marriage, as thereafter the husband would be responsible for the maintenance of his wife and child. For example in July 1820:-

Petworth constable for taking J Pannell	£1.10s.0d.	£1.50
Self & Constable to Petworth to fetch Pannell	£1.10s.0d.	£1.50
Licence and Ring	£4. 0s.0d.	£4.00
Parson & Clerk for marrying Pannell and Bennett	15s.0d.	75p
Dinner for them	3s.6d.	18p

Both signed the Marriage Register with a cross.

Entry in Shere Parish Marriage Register, 1820

The overseers also managed to identify and charge the absent fathers on some occasions. In October 1820, for example:- 'Expences of self & Mansell going to Lymington after Joseph Drodge for Rebecca Stanfords child £3 18s. 6d (£3.93)' and in the summary accounts for the year 1820-21; 'Cash of Drodge for a Bastard £15.' The same account shows the total of £90 recovered from three other fathers.

At a Court Baron, the manor court of Gumshall Netley, on the 26th November 1819 it was agreed that twenty acres of land adjoining the workhouse should be inclosed for a garden:-

> Whereas the said Manor lies partly in the Parish of Shere and partly in the Parish of Ewhurst in the said county of Surrey And whereas it is apprehended it will be very advantageous to the Inhabitants of the said Parish of Shere if an Inclosure is made of twenty acres of Land part of the Waste of this Manor lying in or near Pislake Bottom in the said Parish of Shere and if the same is added to the Workhouse there belonging to the said parish of Shere to be employed for the use of the said Parish . . .

First Page of Inventory of Shere Workhouse 1836

Early in the following year there was sustained activity related to clearing the ground. Men were employed at 1s 8d.(9p) a day for ditching, draining, banking, grubing (grubbing), cutting heath and paid for loads of roots and planting potatoes. This does seem to have been a positive approach to managing the increased numbers of able-bodied men.

The Vestry held a meeting twelve years later in April 1832 to consider extending the work and the 'propriety of taking Land or inclosing Waste Lands for the use of the Poor of the Parish' but their conclusions are not recorded.

The inventory of workhouse contents just before the last inmates were moved out in 1836 is written in a florid hand; it lists 'stump bedsteads', meaning those without headboards, flock mattresses, sheets, feather beds, coverlets, blankets, rugs and bolsters which indicates some degree of comfort. The bottoms of the bedsteads were of sacking, though there is one corded four post bedstead and mattress; there were 'turn-up' bedsteads, folding ones that could be brought out when needed; oak clothes chests; 'earthen chambers' and a night stool for indoor relief at night. There is no indication as to segregation of sexes or ages. Meals were served in the Hall, with the residents sitting up to a 'large 15 feet Dining Table' on forms or stools, eating off wooden trenchers; spoons are mentioned, but not knives and forks. There was a clock, which needed winding daily and repairing at intervals, and The Table of Rules; also a Bible and two testaments and 'A Large Volume of Acts of Parliment'.

Brewing was done on the premises and there was also a bakehouse. In many respects it would seem that the inmates were better off than those struggling to maintain themselves and their families from small and irregular wages outside.

Pressures on the Old Poor Law

As long as men are men, a poor society cannot be too poor to find a right order of life,
nor a rich society too rich to have need to seek it.
'The Acquisitive Society'
R.H.Tawney.

The years immediately after the Napoleonic Wars ended in 1815 were a period of great difficulty nationally and particularly in the agricultural counties. There were poor harvests in 1816 and 17 and returning soldiers and militiamen added to the numbers of men looking for work. The end of the war brought an expectation of better times, but this was not realised. High wheat prices which had caused hardship to the poor had brought prosperity to the farmers; when wheat prices fell without a corresponding drop in the price of bread, there was an increase in the able-bodied poor as farmers felt the pinch and reduced the number of men they employed. Those assessed to pay the poor rate came under severe pressure.

In Shere collection and expenditure for the year 1817-18 reached a peak of £1,929.8s.2d. (£1,929.41) contributing to the record national total of £9.3m. in that year. It must be admitted, however, that price inflation was rife during the war years as a contemporary economist explained, 'The total rise in prices during the war appears to have been between 60 and 70 per cent., £160 or £170 being required in 1813 to make the purchases, whether for the necessaries, comforts or luxuries of life , which were made in 1792 for £100.' Divers strategies were applied nationally in an attempt to manage the problem of excess labour, some of which were practised in Shere. The Speenhamland system, mentioned above, was one. Of the three other practices, the Labour Rate was not imposed, the Roundsman System was tried and the use of parish labour on the roads was common.

The Labour Rate entailed a separate rate assessed on the usual property qualifications, with employers either paying the rate in money or employing a number of labourers to match their assessment. The Roundsman System offered able-bodied pauper labourers employment in turn and those taken on would have their wages subsidised from the Poor Rate.

The Shere Vestry set out the arrangements they wished to put in place:-

Persons renting	£50 p^r Annum & under to employ a man:	1 week
	£50 & under £100	2 weeks
	£100	3 weeks
	£150	4 weeks

By order of the Vestry July 31st 1816.

It does not explain whether this order should be repeated, but in 1816-17 eighteen ratepayers took part, employing seventeen men for periods of six days at a time. George Bowbrick was engaged for ten periods of six days, most of the others for only one. There are various comments, such as 'was not employed', 'did not go, got another job', and 'would not employ him'. This effort cannot have made a great impact on the numbers of men seeking relief (70 in 1816-17) or perhaps the recording was deficient. Work on the roads is recorded routinely in the account books under such items as 'digging gravel', 'digging ditch in Gumshall Marsh' in 1816; '9 men picking stones', 'pd for load of stones', 'moving stones' and '27½ rods of road in Hound House Hollow' in 1817. Wages paid to the poor for this work were 1s.(5p) a day in 1820, with boys being paid half the amount.

19th century photograph of man picking stones.

The 1820s were a period of accelerating change and public debate. Population was growing all over the country, from six to nine millions during the second half of the eighteenth century and from nine to fourteen millions by 1831; mechanisation was creeping in to agriculture as well as in industry; new concepts and theories were being bandied about. This period was strongly influenced by the thinking of Adam Smith, whose *Wealth of Nations* came out in 1776 and T. Robert Malthus whose *Essay on the Principle of Population* was first published in 1798. Under the liberal individualistic view of Smith's theory of natural liberty, 'the poor, as much as the rich, were free, responsible, moral agents . . . free to establish their claim to higher wages, a higher standard of living, a higher rank in life'. The corollary to this was that those who failed to improve their situation by their own efforts had only themselves to blame if they remained in poverty and dependent on others. T. Robert Malthus was thought to be living in Albury in a detached part of the parish of Shere in the 1790s, and serving as curate to the chapel at Oakwood in the neighbouring parish of Abinger. He is mentioned in William Bray's Diary as a visitor to his house in Shere. His concern that population would outrun the means of subsistence and the need for checks to population growth meant that he led a body of opinion which objected to the practice of subsidising wages from the poor rates on the grounds that it would encourage the poor to breed. His was the loudest and most enduring voice, but there were other contemporary writers including the economist Joseph Lowe, who suggested that increased population led to greater consumption and prosperity.

Although expenditure on Poor Relief in Shere parish fell from its peak in 1817, expenditure remained consistently higher than before the wars, even allowing for inflation. The Vestry was diligent in devising ways of finding employment for the poor and the local rate payers seemed prepared to support its demands. By 1830 the number of inmates in the workhouse had fallen back to 20 from 44 in 1819 and the rate per head to 3/6 (17p) rather than the 4/-(20p) which applied from 1810 through to 1821.

In spite of increased demand on the Poor Rate the Parish Officers were prepared to spend money on items of clothing for its poorer members; for example under 'Orders' in the Vestry Book of May 3rd. 1818:-

Widow Bakers Boy. Stuff for a Round Frock a Shirt and a Pair of Linings
Jas Harrisons Boy. Stuff for a Round Frock
Plaws Boy. a Shirt and a pair of Stockings
Cumbers Boy. a pair of Leather Breeches and a Round Frock
Allens Girl to go to James Smallpeices from the Workhouse
till further orders

There was an order on June 1st for 2 round frocks, a swanskin jacket, a pair of breeches, 2 shirts, 2 pair of stockings and 2 neck handkerchiefs and a hat, perhaps to maintain the stock of goods available and also a hat and a swanskin waistcoat for James Jones. A 'round frock' is more commonly known as a smock and swanskin is 'a twilled flannel with a downy surface used by working men for trouser linings'.

A Surrey smock of about 1860

Another item of expenditure which might seem over-generous at such a time, concerned James Tickner. He was allowed £5 for 'Sea bathing at Margate' in October 1821. This rather startling entry comes between routine business such as 'Widow Loveland & 3 children £1.0.0.' and '8 Bearers for Gates's Corpse 8s.(40p)'. Whatever the complaint, the treatment proved efficacious as in September 1823 Mr Hexter, Surgeon of Dorking, was offered 'the sum of £5.10s. (£5.50) as a compensation for the cure of James Tickner at Margate'. It seems that Tickner's original £5 should have been paid direct to Mr Hexter.

Paragraph from Shere Vestry Book, 1823

In many other parts of the country, however, the situation was not so well under control. Towns were experiencing rapid expansion and population increase and could not manage the escalating demands. Assessment for rates was still confined to property, not to other sources of wealth. There were reports of cruelty to workhouse inmates as some governors put part of the meagre allowances into their own pockets. The presence of the able-bodied pauper, thought to be a man who could have found work if he had made sufficient effort, was perceived as a threat to stability and good order.

This perception was reinforced by a rising of agricultural labourers in the southern counties of England in 1830-31 which gained the name of the 'Captain Swing Riots', as threatening letters were sent to farmers bearing a skull and crossbones under this name, though no one person was ever identified. Their activities included rick burning and machine breaking in a protest against low wages. There are not many recorded incidents in Surrey, as of the total of 1034 listed, only 24 occurred in the county. The village of Albury, however, closely associated with Shere geographically and socially, was mentioned three times, twice for arson against a farmer and once for a riot targeted at an overseer.

This seemed to point to radicalisation under the system of wage subsidies, and the new Whig government established a Royal Commission to investigate Poor Relief in 1832. It was set up at a time when there were those who advocated the total abolition of poor relief. They could quote Malthus, who said 'no person has any right on society for subsistence, if his labour will not purchase it' and also stress the fact that the neighbouring countries of France, Germany and Ireland had no such system. Those who recognised that abolition was not viable suggested positive reforms such as 'parochial development of schools, allotments, and self help agencies', but the proposal which proved the most popular was that of a 'deterrent workhouse', a multi-purpose establishment:-

'. . . before we can enforce discipline so as to control the vicious and refractory, we must provide a place of refuge as well as restraint . . . Let the system of management ensure every tenderness towards the infirm, the aged and the guiltless, while it imposes wholesome restraint upon the idle, the profligate, the refractory . . .'

Thus members of the 'inferior classes' were to be made to appreciate how degrading it was to claim relief and how much better it would be to gain independence by honest industry.

The Commission started its inquiries by sending questionnaires to all the parishes in England and Wales, of which approximately 10% replied. There is no record among the documentary material for Shere that the parish completed one or in the cumbersome report of the Commission, that Shere was included in the one-fifth of total parishes to be visited by an Assistant Commissioner.

The whole thrust of the Commissioners' report was that the system of out-relief which subsidised wages and gave allowances to families in their own homes was to be severely curtailed. In its place, Union Workhouses were to be built to serve several parishes, and relief would be conditional on entering the workhouse, which was to be 'less eligible', that is less comfortable, than conditions outside.

The New Poor Law

We are not concerned with very poor, they are unthinkable, and only to be approached by the statistician or the poet.
'Howards End'
E.M.Forster

The New Poor Law attempted to apply a centralised, standardised, rule driven system on an institution which had grown over two centuries to provide local, empirical, variable solutions to the problem of poverty.

However, there is no doubt that by the late 1820s the system was becoming overloaded and new thinking was needed. Poor rates for England and Wales had escalated from £5.3m. in 1802-03 to £9.3m. in 1817-19 and after a reduction in the early 1820s had risen again to £8.6m. in 1831-32 and 1832-33. The Commissioners appointed in 1832 to investigate and review the operation of the Poor Law recruited 26 Assistants to travel the country and report back on their findings. They also circulated *Town Queries* and *Rural Queries* to the parishes for comment. Admirable as these efforts might appear, it would seem that the response to these questionnaires was low and as the science of investigation was new, the questions were ambiguous and the answers difficult to analyse; in fact no real analysis was attempted and the Commissioners were guilty of extracting the evidence that would support their theories. They firmly believed that the cause of the problem of increased spending on the Poor Law was 'a system which relieved mere poverty (rather than destitution) . . . and that the greatest source of abuse is outdoor relief afforded to the able-bodied'. The parish of Shere might be thought guilty in this respect.

The two authors of the report on which the Poor Law Amendment Act was based, Edwin Chadwick and Nassau Senior, were intent on putting Utilitarian principles into action. They wanted to control excess expenditure but more particularly, to impose order on a random situation. Their report was based on the concept that out-relief was a cause of population growth, under employment and low wages, whereas recent research suggests that it was a response.

The recommendations of the report were that in future the parish was no longer to be the unit of administration, although poor rates would continue to be levied at parish level. Parishes would be grouped together into Unions, based on a town central to the group. Paupers were to be separated into four categories: the aged and impotent, children, able-bodied males and able-bodied females. Existing workhouses were to be adapted and used if possible, otherwise new Union Workhouses could be built. Administration would be vested in a Board of Guardians for each Union, elected on a property qualification and with representation from the parishes; magistrates would be *ex-officio* members. All would be responsible to the Poor Law Commissioners at Somerset House in London and could take few independent decisions. Out-relief could only be granted in exceptional circumstances. Finance for building the new workhouses would be raised through applying the money from the sale of parish properties, with loans being made available to bridge the gap.

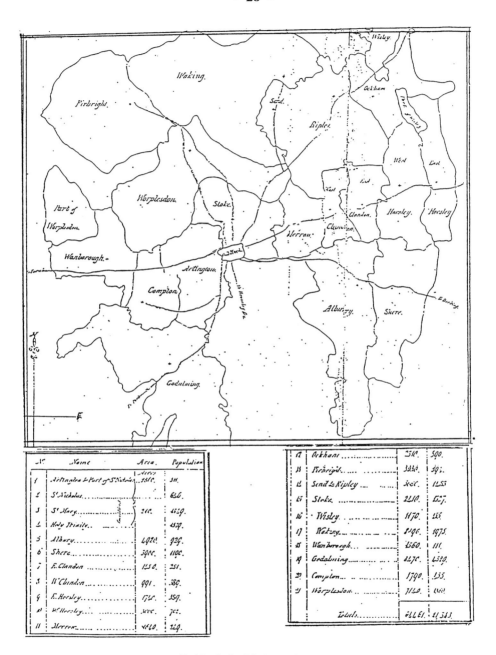

Parishes in the Guildford Union

In England and Wales 15,000 parishes were amalgamated to form some 600 Unions. Twenty one parishes went to make up the Guildford Union, lying in an arc from Godalming south west of the town, through Pirbright to Woking and Wisley in the north, East Horsley and Shere on the east and Albury to the south. The combined population of the parishes in the Union was 21,343.

After considering the possibility of using the existing workhouses at Worplesdon and Godalming, (the Vestry at Godalming was strongly in favour of this), the Guildford Board of Guardians decided that a new Union Workhouse at Guildford would be necessary to accomodate the expected numbers. The architect George Gilbert Scott, a young man at the beginning of a distinguished career, was approached by Edwin Chadwick, Secretary to the Poor Law Commissioners concerning a design for the Guildford Union Workhouse. He replied on March 18th 1837 apologising for the delay in answering the letter and stating 'that the number of persons to be accomodated is 300, the Estimate £4,700'.

Foot of letter from George Gilbert Scott, March 18th 1837

Scott's partner, W.B.Moffat, produced the plans for the proposed Guildford Union Workhouse which were well received by the Board of Guardians. The figure quoted above must be for the building only and not the total cost which would include fitting out. In August 1837 a list was prepared to show the required contribution of each parish and the 'calculated cost of Union Workhouse was stated to be £6,000'. The amount to be paid by Shere was £477.5s.0d. (£477.25). The churchwardens and overseers of Shere had some problems with the sale of the parish workhouse, owing to the copyhold tenure of the workhouse site and to the fact that seventeen acres of land and two cottages which were freehold had been added to the original property. This occasioned considerable correspondence between them and the Poor Law Commissioners at Somerset House. The properties were finally sold in March and April 1838 in three lots. The sale of the workhouse raised £304.3s.8d. (£304.19).

Public opinion was not wholly behind the new administration of the Poor Law. *The Times* thundered at some length in the editorial of 19th April 1834, welcoming the effort to reduce 'waste of funds in affording relief to able-bodied paupers and the part payment of wages to farm Labourers from the Poor Rates'; but it also sounded a note of caution about 'the mode so rigorous and undiscriminating' of conditioning relief to entry to the workhouse. In rounded terms it asked: 'may not cases occur in which the inexorable adherence to such a regulation would be equivalent in point of cruelty to a denial of all relief. Is the casual pauper whom a scanty supply might relieve and set at profitable work to be taken as a matter of course from his family and consigned to a virtual prison?'

It gave qualified approval to the simplification of the Settlement Laws so that settlement would depend on birthplace only, and applauded the fact that 'the law of bastardy is substantially amended by throwing the support of the illegitimate child upon the vicious mother', (and thus exposed its prejudices). It reached its peroration with a warning and a question about accountability, querying the wisdom of the 'institution of a central board invested with formidable powers and one of them the expenditure at its own discretion of enormous sums of public money. Is this board of unconstitutional power really necessary? . . . we warn the House of Commons to consider well the necessity for such an establishment which, for aught that yet appears, is not to be responsible to any acknowledged tribunal'.

A strongly worded comment, published after four years experience of the operation of the New Poor Law, appeared in the protest pamphlet *The Poor Man's Friend* of April 1838, subtitled with some irony 'Blessings of the New Poor Law'. The first sentence reads: 'The combination of wealth against poverty in the Poor Law Bill, was one of the most extraordinary instances of successful despotism that ever graced or disgraced the annals of English History'.

THE POOR MAN'S FRIEND.

BLESSINGS OF THE NEW POOR LAW.

Price One Penny, or 7s. per Hundred for Distribution.

THE combination of wealth against poverty in the Poor Law Bill, was one of the most extraordinary instances of successful despotism that ever graced or disgraced the annals of English history; and when it is considered that such pretended friends to the poor as Mr. Hume and his coadjutors—such mock patriots as had for years cajoled the working classes—were among the supporters of that disgusting measure, where can the poor look for friends? cost Mr. Hetherington, the proprietor, years of labour and loss and while two public-spirited individuals worked incessantly for the cause in their different ways, each steadfastly maintaining the interests of the poor, they were gradually impoverishing themselves, without the prospect of re-action; and, conscious of his right to be supported, each was reluctant to give up his task while the slightest hope remained. The consequence was, as

Masthead of protest pamphlet *The Poor Man's Friend*

It then listed the principles of the new law as it appeared to the authors:-

It removed from ratepayers the control of expenditure of their money and gave it to 'three extravagantly paid commissioners' This was thought to be a ' direct infringement upon the liberty of the subject'.

It reduced 'the most respectable unfortunates in the kingdom to the same misery and privation as the most hardened criminals and vagabonds'.

It took 'children from parents and husbands from wives - breaking the spirit of the aged by severing the strongest ties - paying no respect to persons - depriving the few declining years of the reduced, the sick, and the disabled, of all comfort, by refusing the solace of that society which could alone soften the bitter pangs of affliction'. Men and women were to be segregated, even if man and wife.

It demanded attendance at religious services of the Established Church thus denying freedom of worship to those of other denominations and 'depriving them of the comfort of religion when approaching the end of their earthly sufferings'. There was a church of England chapel in every Union Workhouse but no provision for any other faith.

It visited 'the villainy of the seducer upon the victim of his seduction', thus expressing the opposite view to that of *The Times*

The pamphlet is illustrated by lurid engravings showing some of these abuses, including one of the Beadle carrying off children (which graces the front of this booklet) and another of a pauper child asking for more soup. Charles Dickens' *Oliver Twist* was published between 1837 and 1839 and used both of these images.

Engraving from *The Poor Man's Friend*

Copies of this publication were distributed in Guildford to the alarm of the men of the Town, and the Clerk to the Poor Law Union wrote to the Poor Law Commissioners in some agitation:-

Gentlemen, Last Thursday week three miserable looking men came into this Town hawking pamphlets (one of which is inclosed) about the streets for sale - one of the men beating a drum to attract notice - the Police and men of the Town thinking the proceedings ought not to be allowed took the three men into custody and brought them before the Mayor - His Worship on looking at the Publication deemed it to be of a very mischievous character and tending to prejudice the minds of the lower orders against the new Poor Law . . .

The Mayor confiscated the papers and confined the men in the magistrate's office but:-

On the following Sunday there appeared a Paragraph in the *Guide* and *London Dispatch* newspapers intimating that legal proceedings would be taken against the Mayor and his Officers for unlawfully taking the Men into Custody and detaining their Papers.

The Poor Law Commissioners were not impressed by the importance of the incident, but were concerned at the risk of expense. They suggested that the sale of pamphlets might have 'constituted an unlawful hawking or the noise of the drum constituted such a disturbance as to justify the taking of the men', but the papers were not so offensive to good morals as 'to justify detention and there was a grave risk of incurring serious legal costs of which the possibility of recovering any is in doubt'.

The Times may have had justified anxieties about the lack of accountability of the Poor Law Commissioners and the *Poor Man's Friend* justified concern about abuses suffered by the poor, but the majority of magistrates and Guardians, who were drawn from the land owning fraternity, felt they were co-operating in a system that would reduce poor rates and curb the numbers of 'undeserving' poor.

There is no doubt of the different level of provision for the poor in Shere parish before and after the Act came into force. The Shere Select Vestry did their best to tighten up administration, but out-relief formed a large proportion of their expenditure. Their Resolution Book in 1830 laid out quite clearly what it was prepared to do on its first page. It resolved:- '1st That the Overseers immediately prepare separately Lists of Persons who have received Regular and Occasional relief since Christmas Day last together with a Report of the Grounds on which persons have been relieved. 2dly That persons applying for relief shall be required to produce a note from their Employers stating the amount of their earnings respectively for the preceding Fortnight.   signed Edm^d Lomax Chairman'.

It also resolved to hold a meeting to discuss regulating the pay of the paupers. This meeting was held at *The White Horse*, Shere on February 1st 1830, when it was decided that the opportunity for paid labour on the roads should be given firstly to married men and women 'neither earning anything' and adjusted for family size. The sums involved were not very large:-

Man & Wife & 2 children neither earning anything, per day   1/6   8p
Man and Wife & 1 child   1/4   7p
Man and Wife   1/2   6p
That no single Men or Boys be put on the road except on particular circumstances

That relief be given as follows:-

A man and wife having more than two children & neither child ear[n]ing anything 1s.(5p) per week per head for the third child and 1/6(7p) per week per head for all the rest. That Day Labour on the Land should be 1/8(9p) per Day. That no notice be taken of a man's ear[n]ing . If in work it is to be considered he earns 10s.(50p) per Week. Those paupers living in Parish Houses & where the Parish guarantee the rent a deduction of 1s.(5p) per week should be made on those having house without garden and 1/6 (7p) with Garden. This plan being liberal it must be understood by the Paupers that they are not to apply for relief for weather or any other caserale [casual] case but in urgent cases such as long illness for want of work and in all such cases a note to be brought from Master or Doctor. signed Rowland Goldhawk

This indicates an effort to organise payment of relief in a more systematic fashion, and there are still the familiar entries concerning individual names, granting money for rent, relief in illness, casual work, midwifery and burial expenses. It does, however, resolve that 'no Relief whatever to be allowed to Paupers who keep a Dog (except shepherds)'.

An Account of Moneys Disbursed by the Overseers of the Parish of Shere from 1832-1833 shows the total amount collected and paid out during the year as £3,027.2s.4½d. (£3,027.12); a contrast to the total of £380.2s.4¾d. (£380.12) in 1776-77 and £113.19s.3d. (£113.96) in 1711-12.

Although the Poor Law Amendment Act became law in 1834 the transfer of responsibilities was gradual as a complicated system of bureaucratic inspection and control had first to be put in place. Thus the practice of allowing generous amounts to equip girls and boys for service or apprenticeship continued in the parish of Shere, as on May 13 1835 a request was granted to John Freeloves daughter Hannah for 'cloathes for service; 1 pair of Stays, Gown, 2 Peticoats, 2 pairs of stockings, 3 Aprons, Handkerchief and 2 changes' and when John Ingells applied for 'cloathes for his Son being in Service at Brighton, a Fustian Jacket & Trowsers', it was also granted.

Someone was caught out, however, for on Aug 11 1831, 'This day the weekly pay of George Penfold was reduced one shilling & sixpence (7p) on discovery that one of the Daughters had been out at Service one year'.

The items concerning clothes granted in 1835 by officers of the local Vestry contrast starkly with the response to a request made on behalf of 19-year-old William Bignold on 19 June 1838 when the new system was in force. He had been 'an idle lad', transferred back to Shere Workhouse from Bermondsey Workhouse and now had prospect of 'a permanent situation' but needed 10/- (50p) for appropriate clothes. The request went from Shere via the clerk to the Guardians at Guildford to the Poor Law Commissioners in London. The reply was crisp and calculated:-

I think that as the chance of this paupers getting into permanent employment depends on his getting some clothes, the Guardians may be allowed to agree with his employer to find him some to the amount of 10/- (50p) which will be repaid to him if the pauper remains six months in his service.
p.s. I guard the concession in this manner, thinking it probable that his employer only requires his services during the busy period of the next 3 months and may then turn him off.

Perhaps the sentiments of *The Poor Man's Friend* were justified, but equally it might be claimed that the parish officers of Shere had raised expectations too high.

From Parish Workhouse to Union Workhouse

There's no scandal like rags, nor any crime so shameful as poverty
'The Beaux' Stratagem'
George Farquhar 1667-1701

The Shere parish workhouse was on a homely scale, if larger and better built than the hovels of the poor; it was in a rural situation, with opportunity for inmates, if capable, to cultivate the seventeen acres of garden attached to it for that purpose. Two cottages on the site had been brought into use to accommodate the surge in numbers after 1815 which reached a peak of 44 in May 1819.

In contrast, the Guildford Union workhouse, if not as elaborate as some of the so-called 'Pauper Palaces', was large, institutional, urban and built to instil fear and submission. Guildford is six miles from Shere and at the time, the only transport was horseback, the carrier's cart or Shanks's pony.

The Poor Law Commissioners laid down requirements regarding the different categories of poor, their segregation, and the need for secure exercise yards. A chapel had to be provided, and room for a burial ground. After a period of discussion and consultation it was decided that the existing workhouses at Godalming and Worplesdon did not provide sufficient space for the expected numbers, also at one time it was thought that Godalming might leave the Union. The Poor Law Commissioners remained in favour of using the existing workhouses, but the Guildford Guardians at a meeting on 16 July 1836 resolved by a majority of eighteen to four that 'it was expedient to erect a central workhouse'.

There was a period of transition before the Union Workhouse was completed. The first meeting of the new Board of Guardians was held on Tuesday 12th April, 1836 at the old Guildford workhouse, subsequent meetings took place weekly on Saturday mornings at the Abbot's Hospital. Lord King of Ockham was appointed chairman, George Smallpeice of Guildford, gentleman, was to be clerk at a salary of £130 p.a. and Samuel Haydon Esq. was the Treasurer and required to give security to the amount of £2,000. Local magistrates were to be *ex-officio* members. The Board was quick to take action; three areas were designated which would be served by a Relieving Officer and these posts were advertised; the parish representatives were asked to produce lists of all aged and infirm persons receiving out-door relief and also a list of 'the highest number of able-bodied persons who have at any one time during the late winter been receiving out of door relief'.

Instructions and practice in this early period of operation seem to be somewhat at variance. It is quite clearly stated in the minutes of 21st May 1836 'that no relief be given to the non Resident paupers of the Union from and after the first of June next whether able-bodied or otherwise'; while at the same time, the Relieving Officer for Shere, Mr Clarke, was disbursing relief to the amount of £5 3s.6d. (£5.17) in the parish for one week in June, which was approved by the Guardians.

On July 2nd 1836 it was ordered that the Clerk 'write to the Overseers of the several Parishes in the Union instructing them to continue the management of the Poor in their respective Workhouses and Poorhouses as heretofore' and also reminding them that 'it is ordered that no relief shall be given to any able-bodied male pauper on account of Rent'. This order was revised a fortnight later:-

Resolved That the relieving Officers be instructed early in the week after next to remove all the able bodied Men, Women and Children from the respective Workhouses in the Union to the Workhouse at Godalming : That with the exception of the aged and infirm now in the Godalming Workhouse all persons of that Class throughout the Union be removed to the Chapleston Workhouse

From Minute Book of Guildford Board of Guardians

The last entry in the Workhouse Account Book for Shere is for August 4th 1836 which has a list of names of ten men and six women but their subsequent destination is not known.

They were:-

Wm. Creasey	Henery Mansell
George Bubrick	John Rapley
Jas Lucas	Sarah Page
Edward Lambert	Hannah Coles
Thomas Hooker	Ann Goslin
John Coles	Sarah Laurance
William Daniels	Mila May
Jas Moore	Mary Allen

This move seemed a little premature, as a letter to the Poor Law Commissioners from the clerk to the Guildford Board of Guardians reported that 'a large number of Paupers are now congregated in both Worplesdon and Godalming Workhouses without any means of classification whatever'.

There must have been a very uncomfortable and unsettling period for the poor of all the parishes during this transition period. The local workhouses had to be closed and the property sold to raise money for the Union Workhouse. No capital was available from central government for the new construction, only what was forthcoming from the parishes, although loans could be provided from the Exchequer Bill Loan Commission at South Sea House, London.

The contributions of the several parishes are set out in the following table:-

To the Poor Law Commissioners, London   26 August 1837
Gentlemen, From an inspection of the accounts of the Guildford Union for the three years ended 25th March last it appears that the following are the proportions in which the parishes should respectively contribute to the establishment charges of the Union in accordance with which your Order should be issued.

St Nicholas Artington	£ 443
St Mary	£ 417
Holy Trinity	£ 295
Albury	£ 388
Sheere	£ 637
East Clandon	£ 90
West Clandon	£ 165
Merrow	£ 144
Ockham	£ 226
Pirbright	£ 238
Send & Ripley	£ 661
Stoke	£ 610
Wisley	£ 33
Woking	£ 847
Worplesdon	£ 706
Wanborough	£ 46
Godalming	£2098
Compton	£ 180

I have the honour to be etc   Geo. Smallpeice Clerk

Shere's contribution seems to have been exceeded, as a return of August 1838 shows;-

Return of Amounts collected by Shere		
Net produce of Sale [of Workhouse]	£308 3s. 8d.	£308.18
Total Amount already paid	£144 9s. 8d.	£144.48
Sum lent to Guardians	£304 3s. 8d.	£304.18
Amount of Annual Instalments	£30 8s. 0d.	£30.40

The cost of the Guildford Union Workhouse grew in the building, as is common in most such capital projects. The architect's estimate in March 1837 was £4,700, the 'calculated cost' in August of the same year £6,000 and by 1st November 1838 for 'Items already expended and to be expended in the erection of the New Workhouse, including alterations in the Infirmary since the Workhouse became inhabited' the grand total was £8,859 9s. 10d.

If a deterrent effect was planned, it would seem that all the ingredients for deterrence were in place, but the fact that the Union Workhouses filled rapidly points to a wide prevalence of a depth of poverty among the elderly, the sick, and the widows for whom there was no other alternative once out-relief was denied. For the able-bodied man with wife and children, as opposed to the single vagrant, entry to the Workhouse because there was no gainful employment available to him in his parish would seem to be a very negative and expensive solution.

Guildford Union Workhouse, opened 1838

The local officers struggled to do their best for the poor of their parish as they had done in the past, but found it increasingly difficult. There is correspondence from 1837 relating to a neighbouring parish which demonstrates the rigidity of the Poor Law Commissioners' approach. The overseers were concerned with a man and wife and eight children, the eldest a boy of 13 years, whose 'earnings (in total 12s.(60p) a week) are insufficient to maintain them'. The wife was in bad health and the children 'so idle and mischievous that no one will employ them'. They were then receiving four loaves weekly from the parish but 'in consequence of recent order that will cease from 26th [August]'. The Overseers request for continuance of out-relief was supported by a letter from a local landowner who employed the man but he was 'a bad mower' and only took his share with other men in reaping. 'He is to my knowledge so weak from want of proper food that if I had not supplied him with some he must have given up work'. The Poor Law Commissioners' response to this and one other request was stark:-

Regarding the circumstances of the two labourers and the evils attendant upon a departure from the Rule and Sound Principles, the Commissioners are unable to sanction any relief to them except it be afforded in accordance with the Law.

The local Guardians made some attempt to soften this approach, though as these cases had to be referred to the Commissioners it is uncertain how much effect they can have had. At least some expressed concern as on 15 October 1836 it was moved by Mr Foster of the parish of St.Mary, Guildford,'that each Case shall be investigated and decided according to its own merits and that able-bodied labourers out of employment shall not be indiscriminately refused relief out of the Workhouse'. The Motion was carried by 12 votes to six.

There were some exceptions allowed to the Rules concerning out-relief; in June 1839 it was granted to Mary Errett of Shere who 'is the wife of an able-bodied Pauper named John Errett who was transported for seven years a few months ago and she has six children viz. 5 boys aged 11, 9, 4, 3, and 5 months and a girl aged 6 - the women bears a very good character'

In contrast, in the same year 'a woman named Skinner with four children applied for relief, her husband (who is an able-bodied man) having deserted her in consequence of a family quarrel and she is now with her children supported by her Father, a labourer aged 65'. The answer to this request was that 'The Commissioners recommend that they should be relieved in the Workhouse' and continued loftily 'such cases having been found to operate for the prevention of desertion on parts of Husbands and Fathers'.

Separation of husbands and wives from: *The Poor Man's Friend*

The craftsmen and tradesmen of the villages appeared to be weary of the administrative burdens they had carried for so long, and it became hard to recruit men prepared to be overseers with the prospect of bureaucratic intervention. A letter of 1835 sums it up:-

> The Rate Payers complain flour is very cheap
> - Rates very high - an overseer scarcely to be found

and even a paid collector did not solve the problem, as a letter from the Auditor to the Board of Guardians shows :-

> To the Board of Guardians of the Guildford Union
> My Lord and Gent[n], I beg to acquaint you that on calling for the Quarterly Statements of the Overseers of the several parishes of the Union for the Quarter ending the 25th March last I have had considerable difficulty in obtaining and passing any satisfaction from the parish of Shere arising principally from the inefficiency of the salaried Rate Collector to perform an Accountants Duty - It unfortunately happened also that the acting overseer for the past year could not write therefore the Collector could derive no assistance from that officer.
> As the parish of Shere is very extensive and the Duties arduous I have thought it necessary to report the fact to the Board and take the Liberty of recommending the Board to require the parish to appoint a competent Collector of the Rates unless the Overseers choose to perform the Duties themselves.

> Your most obedient Servant,   J.Rand, Auditor

The Parish of Shere in 1841

The best of all would be a person who has all the good things a poor person has and all the
good meals a rich person has, but that's never been known.
'The Matchmaker'
Thornton Wilder

The preceding chapters have attempted to show some of the changes which took place in rural life from the reign of George I to the beginning of the Victorian era, illustrated by examples from the parish of Shere. During the whole period care was provided in the community for its vulnerable members in a practical and organised manner, in accordance with the law.

It could be said that the parish provided a welfare state in miniature; there was regular support for single mothers, and efforts were made to trace the absent fathers and charge maintenance; the elderly and the widows were cared for over long periods with payment of rent and regular weekly allowances and the support of a neighbour to tend them in sickness. After death, laying out and burial fees could be covered so there was no anxiety on that score. The sick could call on medical attendance, with a doctor retained to attend them in illness and injury, to vaccinate against smallpox and treat those succumbing to the disease; doctors bills could be subsidised. A midwife was available for delivering the babies, and accommodation was possible at the workhouse for a mother's lying-in period if she had nowhere else to go. The homeless traveller was given temporary shelter and relief. The payment of out-relief applied to parishioners living away if their settlement was proven in Shere, and they could continue to claim over many years in spite of the administrative load it placed on the overseers. In the crisis years of 1800 - 1801 extra food was provided in addition to routine measures of relief. Apprenticeship for children was arranged and they were fitted out appropriately.

For the first three decades of the nineteenth century the parish officers continued to carry out their duties, now faced with the intractable problem of the able-bodied man unable to find work, or even if in work, unable to earn enough to support his family. The scale of the problem grew larger as the population of the parish expanded from 871 in 1801 to 1190 in 1831. Initiatives were taken to try to provide work, though a few days in a month at 1s.(5p) or 1/8 (9p) per day cannot be classed as a living wage. Pressures on the parish for out-relief and for the maintenance of paupers in the workhouse continued, although it began to ease a little after 1820. The Paupers Ledger of 1827-1836 shows that many families were in need; in 1830 there were 33 families with 148 children between them classed as 'Pauper Families'. One family at least got away, as Vestry Clerk John Higgins wrote to the Poor Law Commissioners on the 17th April 1835 to say that 'John Wood, a pauper of ours, wishes with his wife and family (4 children) to Emigrate to America the wife being quite agreeable, he has collected by subscriptions to the amount of £22, the passage money for such a family will amount to £34. Would it be legal for the Parish to pay out of the Poor's Rates the remaining £12?' The Commissioners agreed to this request.

It is difficult to present a balanced opinion on the effects of the Poor Law Amendment Act and the operation of the New Poor Law. The politicians, economists and above all, the Poor Law Commissioners, thought they were combatting abuses, reducing public expenditure and providing a better service; there was also a fear of uncontrollable forces. The Assistant Poor Law Commissioner for Sussex wrote, concerning the design of a proposed workhouse, 'Most of the rougher description of paupers will be at work on the Yards and from their Characteristic ferocity will require a vigilant and determined taskmaster'.

The voices raised in opposition quoted individual cases of hardship and played on the emotions. There seemed to be no attempt to analyse the effect on the poor in their parishes after such very drastic changes had been put into effect. The fact that poor rates fell was considered sufficient justification. The effect on workhouse inmates was not so much material deprivation as institutionalisation and depersonalisation. Dread of the workhouse, particularly among the elderly, was still a potent memory into the twentieth century.

In Shere, poor rates continued to be levied to pay for Shere paupers in the new Guildford Union Workhouse, but there was still local expenditure on behalf of the poor.

A ticket of 1836 to enable widow Farley to collect flour from Mr. Southon, signed R.B. (Richard Buchanan, Overseer)

There is a record of large loaves being allotted to 112 names on 24 December 1838, perhaps financed from local charities. Without regular payments, rent subsidies and money for special needs it seems inevitable that low standards of living fell even further. It must also have changed social relationships in the village. It would be one thing to approach the Vestry for help and find familiar, local faces, knowing decisions were made on the spot and that recourse to the Magistrate was possible to challenge their decision; quite another to have one's request considered by the Board of Guardians in Guildford, whose chairman was a lord and other members bore the county gentry names.

Once the new system had settled down, however, and inspection from the Poor Law Commissioners was found to be infrequent, some Boards of Guardians risked making their own decisions. It was more convenient for landowners to pay out-relief to agricultural labourers in slack seasons than to send them to the workhouse and be denied their labour at busy times of the year.

The Labourer's Plight, from G. Mitchell's *The Skeleton at the Plough*

The social composition of the parish of Shere was beginning to change although the rural occupations listed in the first chapter still predominated in 1841.

In the Census returns of that year, the parish is divided into a western and an eastern registration district. The latter covers Gomshall, Peaslake and the hamlets of Sutton, Hoe, Felday and Pitland Street and retained the rural character of the previous century. All the crafts mentioned before are represented with the exception of the weaver, the thatcher and the collarmaker. New occupations were a general dealer, a grocer, a collier (a charcoal seller) and a sweep; early signs of 'service industries'. There were also a lawyer, an independent minister and a schoolmistress. The most common entry was agricultural labourer, 75 men were classed as such out of a total of 738 persons, and they would be the ones, with their families, from whom the poor of the parish came. There were 141 inhabited houses, so average household size was over five. There was still stability in the parish (or lack of enterprise); only 2.5% of the total were born outside its boundaries.

The Western registration district contained the village of Shere, Netley House, the seat of the Shallett Lomax family, and outlying houses and farms. It is interesting that the number of agricultural labourers (49) is less than the combined total of male servants (16) and female servants (41) and that there were 23 people classed as 'Independent'. Of the 609 persons in this Western district, 12% were born outside the parish; it would seem that those employing personal resident servants preferred them to come from elsewhere.

The Rate Assessments of 1840, however, do not indicate a very changed social structure from that of 1711. The total number assessed to pay the poor rate was 112 and of those, five were designated 'esquire'. In addition there were 61 occupiers of property who were not charged; they were 'allowed on account of poverty'.

Conditions in the agricultural counties remained very depressed for some years after 1838. In Shere parish, being part of Surrey and not remote from the capital, other changes were just over the horizon; the Redhill to Reading railway, via Dorking and Guildford, opened in 1849 with a station at Gomshall and brought the first London commuters. Their big houses and gardens offered a new and different kind of employment with related service industries which required a new kind of deference.

No longer would a man who was 'very poor and impotent' feel able to challenge the decision of the overseers as Edward Gates did in 1831;

Form signed by Henry Drummond J.P. 1831

or a woman, a widow and one of the 'Poor of the Parish' write in confidence of a quick response:-

'Gentlemen of the Parish of Shear i shul thenk you to send my Pay as i am in Distress for it shuld be great ley oblig to you if you wil be so kind'.

Notes on Sources

Abbreviations

HRO	Hampshire Record Office
PRO	Public Record Office, Kew
RHC	The Rural History Centre, University of Reading
SAC	Surrey Archeological Collections
SLSL	Surrey Local Studies Library, Guildford
SRO	Surrey Record Office, Kingston-upon-Thames
SRO GMR	Surrey Record Office, Guildford Muniment Room

Sources for 'The Parish of Shere in 1711'

Replies from the parishes to letter from the Bishop of Winchester 1725 HRO 21 M65 B4/1/3
Correspondence between Poor Law Commissioners and Clerk to Guildford Union Board of Guardians 1838 PRO MH12/12333
Transcript of Parish of Shere Burial Register 1691-1812 SRO GMR
Parish of Shere Overseers Account Books and Assessments 1776-1807 and 1810-1821 SRO P/10 1.2.3. and SLSL Microfilm 1042238-9
Summary of Censuses of Great Britain 1801 and 1831 SLSL 314
John Richardson *The Local Historian's Encyclopedia* Historical Publications 1986 ed.

Sources for 'The Old Poor Law'

W.E.Tate, *The Parish Chest,* 3rd ed. Cambridge 1983
Overseers' Account Book SLSL 1042238
Vestry Book SRO GMR PSH/SHER 10/4
Eric Kerridge *Textile Manufactures in Early Modern England* Manchester University Press 1985
O.Manning & W.Bray *History & Antiquities of the County of Surrey* Vol.I 1804 reprinted 1974
K.D.M.Snell *Annals of the Labouring Poor* C.U.P. 1985
Letter from William Cobbett to Mr Gooch, quoted in J.L. & Barbara Hammond *The Village Labourer 1760-1832* 1911 ed. Alan Sutton 1987
Peter Wood *Poverty and the Workhouse in Victorian Britain* Alan Sutton 1991
J.M.Stratton & Jack Houghton Brown *Agricultural Records AD 200-1977* ed. Ralph Whitlock John Baker 1978
Joseph Lowe *The Present State of England* 1823 Augustus M.Kelley New York reprint 1967
Table of Weekly Allowances 1801 SRO GMR PSH/SHER 31/1
Form for transfer of pauper under Settlement Act SRO GMR PSH/SHER 17/20
Case of Militia Family SRO GMR PSH/SHER 37/12
Correspondence of Widow Stocker SRO GMR PSH/SHER 28/2/5

Sources for 'The Shere Workhouse'

Sir Jack Sutherland Harris 'Outline of a Study at Shere on the Identification and History of Village Houses and their Inhabitants c.1500-1850' in *Surrey History* Vol.I. No.I Phillimore 1973
W.E.Tate *The Parish Chest*
H.E.Malden 'Answers made to the Visitation Articles of Dr.Willis, Bishop of Winchester, from the Parishes of Surrey 1724-25' in *SAC* Vol. XXXIX (1931)
Vestry Book SRO GMR PSH/SHER 10/4
Ann Williams 'Albury Workhouse' in *Surrey History* Vol.I No.2 Phillimore 1974

Overseers' Account Book SLSL 1042239
Manor of Gomshall Netley SRO GMR 85/13/704
The Inventory of Shere Workhouse SRO GMR PSH/SHER/30

Sources for 'Pressures on the Old Poor Law'

Mark Blaug 'The Myth of the Old Poor Law and the Making of the New' in the *Journal of Economic History*
Vol.XXIII No.2 June 1963
Joseph Lowe *The Present State of England* 1823, reprinted Augustus.M.Kelly New York 1967
Parish of Shere Vestry Book 1816-1829 SRO P10/1/18
Overseers' Account Book SLSL 1042239
Peter Mandler 'The Making of the New Poor Law *Redividus'* in *Past and Present* No. 117 Nov 1987
B.Stapleton 'Malthus: The Origins of the Principle of Population?' in *Malthus and his Time* Michael Turner ed.
1986
William Bray's Diary SRO GMR 85/1/38
C.W.& P.Cunningham and C.Beard *Dictionary of English Costume* A & C Black 1960 (1976 ed) p.275
Account Book 1821-30 SRO P10/1/5
E.J.Hobsbawm & George Rudé *Captain Swing* Readers Union ed 1970 p.17
Peter Wood *Poverty and the Workhouse in Victorian Britain*
Anne Digby *The Poor Law in Nineteenth Century England & Wales* The Historical Association 1982

Sources for 'The New Poor Law'

Anne Digby *The Poor Law in Nineteenth Century England & Wales*
Peter Wood *Poverty and the Workhouse in Victorian Britain*
Poor Law Correspondence 1834-5 PRO MH/12/ 12332-3
The Times 19 April 1834 Portsmouth Central Library 000140
Vestry Book SRO GMR PSH/SHER 8/1

Sources for 'From Parish Workhouse to Union Workhouse'

Minutes of Meetings of Board of Guardians of Guildford Union 1836-38 SRO BG6/11
Workhouse Account Book, listing inhabitants 1830-36 SRO P10/1/11
Poor Law Correspondence 1834-5 PRO MH12/12332-3

Sources for 'The Parish of Shere in 1841'

Poor Law Correspondence 1834-5 PRO MH12/12332
Mr Hawley's Correspondence PRO MH32/38
Book containing yearly lists of paupers 1830-1835 and account of charity distributed 1838 SRO P10/1/12
Anne Digby *The Poor Law in Nineteenth Century England & Wales*
Census of Great Britain Parish of Shere 1841 SLSL HO 107/1045
Poor Rate Book 1838 SRO P10/1/24
Widow Stocker's correspondence SRO GMR PSH/SHER 28/2/7

Sources for Illustrations
with Acknowledgements and Thanks

- 48 -

Index